LEYLAND BUSES IN ISRAEL

ALON SITON

AMBERLEY

First published 2021

Amberley Publishing
The Hill, Stroud
Gloucestershire, GL5 4EP

www.amberley-books.com

Copyright © Alon Siton, 2021

The right of Alon Siton to be identified as
the Author of this work has been asserted in
accordance with the Copyrights, Designs and
Patents Act 1988.

ISBN 978 1 3981 0574 4 (print)
ISBN 978 1 3981 0575 1 (ebook)

British Library Cataloguing in Publication Data.
A catalogue record for this book is available from
the British Library.

Orgination by Amberley Publishing.
Printed in the UK.

Introduction

This book, which is the first ever written on the subject of Leyland buses in Israel, is dedicated to telling the story of the company's decades-long partnership with the State of Israel. It is the inevitable outcome of a recent discovery in Jerusalem of a large photographic collection showing these beloved buses in service in the small piece of land between the Mediterranean Sea in the west and the Jordan River in the east, which was once governed by Britain itself. Specifically, it describes the warm relationships between the celebrated British automotive manufacturer and Egged, Israel's national public bus company, which for many years was one of Leyland's biggest customers overseas. Triggering a flashback to the author's own happy childhood memories in the 1970s, in the days before the arrival of the mobile phone and the Internet, these old and hitherto unpublished photos are a reminder of a bygone period in Israel's history, when the popular and now sadly nostalgic phrase 'riding the tiger' was for most kids an invitation for a trip aboard a Leyland Royal Tiger bus. In the author's case, it was an opportunity not to be missed to get on Dad's Leyland bus and head out on a week-long tour of the sun-kissed Red Sea shores of the Sinai Desert, or, on a cold and rainy winter day, depart from Tel Aviv on a scheduled long-haul journey to the Sea of Galilee and the Golan Heights, in the far north of the country.

First introduced on a large scale in Israel in the 1950s, the Leylands were phased out in the late 1980s and retired completely, having been replaced with modern German bus models that were built by Daimler Benz and MAN. Some were sold abroad, to developing countries, where they are said to be still running today, but the majority were quietly scrapped and broken up. Fortunately, a few escaped the cutter's torch and are kept in mint condition in Egged's Heritage Center in Holon, a few miles to the south of Tel Aviv, as a living symbol of solid British engineering. For countless Israelis who are old enough to remember the sight and the sound of a Leyland bus in the streets of Jerusalem and Tel Aviv, they provide a chance to go back in time for one more ride on the elderly Tiger. As a tribute to what can only be described as the most durable and reliable buses to have ever run in Israel, this book is offered as a token of admiration and appreciation of that all-terrain workhorse, the Leyland bus.

For his help and support in the making of this book, special thanks are due to Tzvi Weinstock, Head of the Egged Bus Archive, who spared no effort to provide the finest photos and demonstrated a level of knowledge that is rarely found.

The First Buses in British Palestine

In the first post-war years, the common means of transport in British Palestine were as archaic as they were before the British takeover, and usually amounted to a horse-drawn carriage and a camel caravan. The main change was the construction of a new standard-gauge railway line from Egypt to Haifa and Jerusalem, in addition to the existing Turkish narrow-gauge lines, which were heavily sabotaged and largely abandoned already during the war years. With time, and in no small part thanks to the British administration's efforts, a network of paved roads was built throughout the land, at first out of military considerations and, later on, for civilian use. With peace came prosperity and a general improvement in the living conditions. Starting in the 1920s, regular bus services were established between Tel Aviv, Jerusalem, Haifa and Tiberias, as well as local bus routes serving the new Jewish communities in the outlying districts around Tel Aviv. Similar services were started out of Jerusalem to Bethlehem and Hebron and in the opposite direction to Nablus and the Samaria. These services were made possible using trucks that were bought second-hand from the British Army and converted to carry passengers, agricultural products and mail. A temporary solution at best, these primitive trucks were soon replaced with newer and better models with the overall economic growth in British Palestine. Across the border, a trans-desert route was established by the Nairn Company, a pioneering motor transport company that connected Haifa with Beirut, Damascus and Baghdad from 1923 to 1959, using Buick and Cadillac cars and then Marmon-Herrington buses that were actually made of a truck pulling a long Pullman deluxe carriage.

As of 1931, there were four transportation companies on the Tel Aviv–Jerusalem route. 'Hamahir' (literally 'The Rapid') was created in the same year and operated services also to Haifa. 'Hegeh' ('Steering Wheel') was a partnership and the smallest operator on that route. 'Kadima' ('Forwards') and 'The Drivers Union' had each owned a fleet of small vehicles with a workforce of eighty drivers between them. The proliferation of carriers on a single route inevitably resulted in a rivalry which in turn led to endless disputes, financial losses and, over time, a considerable decline in the service standards. When things got out of hand, the matter was brought before the authorities, to the effect that as of 1 January 1933 all four operators became the founding members of a new public bus cooperative named 'Egged', meaning 'a bundle'. It was a brilliant move and from this humble beginning, the new partnership continued to grow and expand to such an extent that it has since then become Israel's national bus company. Egged currently operates one third of all public bus routes in Israel with no fewer than 3,000 modern buses covering a combined daily total of 1 million km. The company's history is tightly linked with that of Israel and even more than that, it is intimately and inseparably connected with Leyland's own story, so much so that for the first forty years after the establishment of the State of Israel, in May of 1948, Leyland's name became synonymous with an Egged bus.

Mention should also be made of Dan, previously Israel's second-largest bus cooperative (since 2002 a private company) and another major Leyland customer. The company was incorporated in 1945 and is mainly active today in the Tel Aviv metropolitan area. As with Egged Tours, so did Dan's tourism subsidiary, United Tours, rely on a fleet of upgraded Leyland buses, which were given an elegant livery of red and white. Finally, many other Leyland buses found their way to private operators both in Israel and the Palestinian Authority, including El Al, Israel's national airline, and local councils, with whom they saw service as school buses.

The Second World War and the State of Israel

The Second World War broke out on 1 September 1939, with Nazi Germany's invasion of Poland and Britain's declaration of war on the Third Reich. Within a short time, the essentially European dispute assumed global proportions, sending shock waves that were also felt in British Palestine, which all at once became a part of a vital supply line of military equipment for the British war effort in North Africa and Syria. The bulk of that challenge was entrusted to the Egyptian and Palestine railways, who received additional locomotives and rolling stock from the War Department. As for buses, the war on Hitler led to a German and Italian blockade on the Mediterranean Sea, creating a severe shortage of rubber tires in British Palestine and the temporary implementation of drastic measures to keep the traffic running at all costs. The situation was bad enough that each bus was allotted no more than six new tires per year, thereby cutting the total scheduled mileage by half and forcing a speed limit of 45 km/h. To make matters worse, the regular maintenance of the buses was similarly affected due to the difficulty of getting a sufficient supply of spare parts. This undesirable situation, which ended along with the war itself, was over in 1945, but by then many of the available buses – a curious mix of petrol-powered American trucks, such as Dodge, Ford and White, that were simply fitted with a locally assembled body – were already showing signs of fatigue and were in any case in need of replacement.

The final three years of Britain's rule in Palestine were a period of political and social chaos brought on by Jewish and Arab terror attacks. Already in 1945, in the face of Britain's unrelenting refusal to let Jewish refugees and survivors of the Nazi persecution into Palestine, Zionist paramilitary organizations joined forces and openly declared war on the British administration and any British civilian and military assets that were present in the country, pending a change in the British policy on Jewish immigration to Palestine. Britain's primary concern at the time appears to have been the possible rise of communism in the Arab world, and political and financial interests dictated a policy that would keep the Arabs on the British side at all costs. Letting more Jews into British Palestine would have alienated the Arabs and the inevitable result was a civil war in the country.

In the morning hours of 14 May 1948, the last British High Commissioner in Palestine, Sir Alan Cunningham, boarded a ship out of Haifa, thereby ending some thirty years of British rule in the Holy Land. That same day in Tel Aviv, at four in the afternoon, David Ben Gurion declared Israel as an independent Jewish state, only to watch the young Israel being cast into a war on all fronts with her neighboring Arab countries. The Arab armies were defeated in the war, although east Jerusalem and the Samaria and Judea regions remained under hostile Jordanian occupation until 1967.

The creation of Israel posed a challenge that, in hindsight, seems to have been almost impossible to overcome. On top of the political problems in the Middle East and the urgent need to secure its borders, Israel had little to go on in its first few years. The available cash reserves were hardly enough to pay for foreign goods, and the economy was unstable after the long war years, the civil war and Britain's departure from the region. Food had to be rationed and to complicate matters even more during a period of austerity, it was necessary to accommodate and cater to the needs of the thousands of newly arrived Jews from Europe, North Africa and Asia. Despite these hardships, a new order was placed in the US with American automotive manufacturers for truck chassis units, to be used in Israel as buses. A first batch was duly built and dispatched to Israel, but the outbreak of war in 1948 had disrupted the order. In the face of an ever-growing demand for more public buses, a new effort was launched to seek a supplier who could deliver such buses in the shortest amount of time, and subject to convenient payment conditions. Thus was born the Chausson Deal, or as it later came to be known, the Chausson Affair.

The Chausson Affair

In the early 1950s, Israel was faced with considerable financial difficulties, which made it nearly impossible to purchase new buses on a large scale abroad. An understanding was arranged with the French government, with American assistance, whereby Israel would receive a shipment of new Chausson buses in exchange for private cars that would be assembled in Israel and then exported to France. The Société des Usines Chausson was a French car parts manufacturer based in the Paris region until 2000. It was originally named 'Ateliers Chausson Frères' after Jules and Gaston Chausson, the two brothers who started the business in 1907, and was involved in the production of Peugeot and Renault car models as well as hundreds of bus bodies for the Paris Transit Authority. The buses-for-cars deal was formally approved and accordingly, Egged was presented with a combined total of 129 Chausson buses for both its long- (fifty seats) and short-haul routes. The first two Chausson buses arrived in 1951 and were soon found to be unfit for service in Israel, first and foremost due to the engine's position, which was right next to the driver's seat. The loud noise, the violent vibration and the immense heat that were constantly generated from the poorly placed engine were bad enough, but worse was yet to come due to serious mechanical defects, extensive corrosion, steering problems and passenger glass windows that tended to crack all too often. An attempt was made to overcome at least some of these problems by replacing the original Somua (a subsidiary of Schneider-Creusot) motors with new ones from Leyland and the Chausson buses were henceforth assigned to local routes to keep them as close to the garage as possible. Despite these efforts, little could be done to save the Chaussons and they were retired and completely disposed of after only a few years in regular service in Israel, having infamously gained the title 'Chausson – Asson', which in Hebrew amusingly translates to 'Chausson – Disaster'. It is worth mentioning here that in the same period, Israel was supplied with a wide range of German-made goods following the September 1952 signing of the Luxembourg Agreement, better known as the Reparations Agreement between Israel and the Federal Republic of Germany, and that at least one offer for new buses was received directly from the long-established, Kassel-based industrial giant Henschel. The company was primarily active in the railway rolling stock market, building locomotives for the West German as well as the global markets, and in the 1950s attempted to gain a foothold in other areas, such as buses and trolleybuses. Henschel's reputation was tarnished due to its unethical conduct during the Third Reich years and it therefore stood little chance of winning a contract in Israel, certainly not in the 1950s, with the memory of the Holocaust still painfully fresh. One cannot help but observe, though, that ordering potentially superior buses from Henschel instead of the inferior ones that arrived from Chausson would have greatly improved the situation in Israel, setting aside the legitimate historical issues, and let alone that other German manufacturers, such as Esslingen and Maybach, were awarded contracts with Israel Railways for the supply of new diesel locomotives and whole trains at exactly the same time and at the Bonn government's expense.

The Leyland Royal Tiger Bus

Of all the seemingly countless bus models that rolled out of Leyland's factory floor, perhaps none is better remembered than the Royal Tiger. A bestseller bus, this popular type was mass produced and exported to many countries around the world, where it often entered service under challenging conditions, and with considerable success. A general description of this bus is therefore in order, given that hundreds of Leyland Tigers were delivered to Israel starting in the 1950s, seventy years ago, with the last surviving units being phased out by 1990, after an impressive career spanning forty years in demanding daily use.

The Royal Tiger was an underfloor-engine bus chassis that was manufactured by Leyland from 1950 to 1954. It sold remarkably well both in Britain and abroad, although the export models differed considerably from the ones that were supplied to British operators. When introduced, it was in fact the fourth version of Leyland's post-war single-deck bus chassis. The Tiger was powered by a mid-frame Leyland motor, coupled to a single-plate clutch and a four-speed gearbox. It set a precedent by becoming the first post-war Leyland bus model that was decorated with the famous Charging Tiger badge, which was also applied to later models such as the Tiger Cub, Worldmaster, Atlantean, Leopard, Lion, Panther and Panther Cub.

By the time production ceased in 1956, a total of 6,500 Tiger units were built. The type was replaced with the lighter Tiger Cub, which entered mass production in 1953 and was well received in Britain. Foreign operators, however, insisted on the original type's proven output and performance, resulting in the introduction of the Leyland Worldmaster model starting in 1954. Another distinctive difference between the British and export models was that the latter had the option of an air-actuated preselector gearbox combination and either air or vacuum brakes. These export Leyland Tigers were particularly in demand in Europe, the Middle East, South America and the Far East. The biggest overseas order for these buses arrived from Cuba, amounting to 620 units for the city of Havana. 450 buses were supplied to Buenos Aires (Royal Tigers and Olympics) and by 1953 Brazil had close to 500 Royal Tigers. Other significant export Royal Tiger orders were received from Australia and New Zealand, Israel, Egypt, Iran, India, Holland, Finland, Spain and Portugal, Kenya, Nigeria, South Africa and Uruguay.

Egged and Leyland

The Chausson calamity was a traumatic experience for Egged, who received the largest share of these dubious French buses and was left to deal on its own with the consequences of that unfortunate incident. Other Israeli operators were similarly eager to dispose of their Chausson buses and this was soon achieved with the appointment of a special Israeli delegation that was sent to Europe on a tour of the continent's bus manufacturers in October to November 1955, with a view on placing a large-scale order for new, diesel engine bus chassis units that would meet the specific requirements of the Israeli market and would also be assembled in Israel. It was in fact the second such tour, with the first taking place already in February to April 1950 and covering Britain, Sweden and Holland, during which the first delegation had the opportunity to thoroughly examine various bus models that were built by Leyland, AEC, Volvo and other European manufacturers during an international exhibition that was held in Amsterdam at the same time.

The second delegation's October 1955 journey to Europe resulted in the publication, in December of the same year, of an official and highly detailed report containing valuable information on the technical, financial and political aspects of its intense dealings with the manufacturers. A relevant and informative document, it is repeated here, in a summarized form, starting with the first meetings in London with the sales representatives and ending with the decision to accept Leyland's offer.

Having reached London, we held a series of business meetings with Leyland, AEC, Daimler and Guy Motors (12-30 October 1955). Our first stop was in Preston for a two-day visit to the Leyland plant there, where we discussed the available models and the technical improvements that would be needed to run the buses in Israel. A similar meeting took place with AEC. On 24 October, we reached Daimler in Coventry and took advantage of the event to visit the Metropolitan Cammell factory in Birmingham. Two days later, on 26 October, we were in Wolverhampton on another meeting with Guy Motors. Our main specifications called for a 150 hp diesel engine, a Wilson 4 speed gearbox, power steering, Westinghouse air brakes, and a cooling system that would be capable of performing in an outside temperature of 42 degrees Celsius. We then left London and travelled to Sweden, where we met with Scania and Volvo at the specific request of the Swedish Government, and with a stop in Copenhagen to see the local transport company's Leyland and AEC buses in action. 04 November saw us in Utrecht (Holland), where we learnt about the benefits of standardization. Our visit to Holland concluded, we noted that the general opinion there was clearly in favor of Leyland and AEC buses.

The delegation also travelled to France, where incredibly it met with Chausson to consider the option of ordering new buses from that manufacturer, only a few years since the Chausson Affair. The visit to Chausson appears to have been sufficiently controversial that prior to the relevant part in the report, a list of pros and cons is given to lay out the reasons for even making the effort to go there. In favor of Chausson were the facts that the company acknowledged its grave mistakes as regards the extremely low quality of the buses delivered to Israel, that it was willing to accept in advance and implement any technical modifications to the basic design, as dictated by the Israeli delegation, and that, in recognition of the above, it was honestly wishing to make amends by generously offering the new buses at a temptingly competitive price. It was also hinted to the distinguished guests that a new deal with Chausson would be politically beneficial thanks to the resulting good impression and the French government's attitude towards Israel. Even more incredibly, the delegation was sold ten Chausson buses as a result of that meeting, under the justification that there were some 200 such buses that were still running in Israel and that this was therefore enough reason to enter into a new deal with the same manufacturer.

The delegation then returned to London, and, after reviewing the various offers, voted in favor of Leyland's proposal. AEC was not amused, it being the third time that their offer was rejected despite a long and exhausting negotiation process with Israel. For this reason, and so as to gather a better experience with the different models, 10 per cent of the total order – fifty buses in all – would have been handed over to AEC. Leyland's response was to threaten the delegation with a price revision, which practically amounted to a penalty in all but name. The Israelis backed down and the first part of the contract, for the purchase of 250 Leyland buses and a shipment of spare parts, was signed on 22 November 1955, sending Leyland into a new era of close cooperation with its customers in Israel. With a longer chassis, the new diesel buses were capable of carrying up to fifty passengers, as opposed to the limited capacity of the previously used petrol-powered trucks. On arrival in Israel, the first Leyland units were prone to overheating and slow braking, but this was solved by installing a bigger engine and an improved cooling system, along with a new type of rear axle and stronger brakes. By 1966, there were enough Leyland buses in Israel that the old petrol trucks were gone.

With Leyland's hold of the Israeli bus market in full swing, in the summer of 1957 a curious turn of events occurred when, on the occasion of Israel's tenth Independence Day celebrations, a decision was made to order new deluxe buses to meet the anticipated rise in tourist traffic. By then, over a thousand Leyland buses had been locally assembled and successfully delivered to Egged and Dan, but the special circumstances called for a change in that policy and already in May 1957, twenty new bus chassis units arrived in Israel – not from Leyland, as may be expected, but from Daimler Motors of Coventry (which was ironically merged into Leyland in 1968). A minor departure from Israel's prevailing agreement with Leyland, Daimler was contracted to deliver its Freeline bus model, which, as with Leyland, was powered by a 150 hp underfloor engine coupled to the Wilson-type gearbox. Ten of the Daimler units were added to Dan's fleet of public buses. The other remaining ten units, which were handed over to Egged, were earmarked for the 1958 celebrations and were accordingly given tourist class bodies. In March 1958, the first two of these locally built deluxe buses, one from Daimler and the other from Leyland, were presented to their prospective new owners. The design incorporated a see-through plastic roof (for better visibility), loudspeakers, fans, and elegant seat covers. Leyland's Super Deluxe version was fitted with reclining seats, reducing their total number to thirty-nine against Daimler's forty-three. These handsome tourist buses saw limited service in the years following 1958, with the last Daimler bus retired in 1971. Happily, one bus, a Leyland Super Deluxe, was wisely preserved and placed in Egged's Heritage Center.

In 1962, Egged and Dan, along with the recently created tourism agent United Tours, took delivery of thirty-six Danish-built, tourist class Leyland buses. The event did not go unnoticed and the local coachbuilders in Israel were quick in rising to the challenge with their own version of a deluxe bus body, which they then marketed to the same operators to the tune of twenty buses in all for Egged. The new bus was taller than the commonly available Royal Tiger, and had a bigger baggage compartment, drop-down passenger windows, plush seats and even an onboard fridge. Outside, a pair of double headlights and chrome covers gave the model a modern look. A hundred units ended up with Egged by 1966.

The need for tourist class buses was relatively modest in Israel's first few years, with only a handful of such buses in 1952, but took off in the late 1950s with the creation of United Tours. Negotiations with DAB (Dansk Automobil Byggeri A/S of Silkeborg, which started collaborating with Leyland in 1953 and as a result relied regularly on Leyland components for its buses until bought by Leyland in the 1970s and renamed Leyland-DAB) commenced in late 1961 and proceeded with such speed that on 28 January 1962, the first ten DAB buses arrived in the Port of Haifa, five each for Egged and Dan, despite protests from the Israeli coachbuilders who were alarmed at what they rightfully perceived as a direct threat on their established links with the bus companies. The objections made little impression on United Tours, who returned to DAB for more of the Danish builder's buses, but appear to have been properly registered with Egged and Dan, who by 1973 bought 310 locally built Leyland units for their tourism operations.

In 1964, along with an order placed in the previous year for 120 new Leyland buses for Dan (which were all assembled in Leyland's new factory in Israel), twenty new and locally built tourist class buses were added to the company's fleet, where they remained in service for the next fifteen years. United Tours was sold to Dan in the late 1970s and the tourist class Leylands were gradually phased out and scrapped.

A new type of the Leyland Royal Tiger bus was launched in Britain in September 1960. The bus, named Lion, was equipped with a modern chassis, a large baggage compartment and power steering, and was 10.4 meters long. Its biggest and most obvious distinction, however, was the location of the 200 hp engine, which was mounted in the rear of the bus, in a protruding fibreglass box that was strangely bulging out of the body outlines. Given Leyland's tight relationships with Israel, it is a little surprising that the Lion bus was first marketed to Egged, prior to the official unveiling in Britain, following a personal visit in June 1959 of an Egged executive to the manufacturer's Lancashire plant, which resulted in the dispatch of two Lions (as chassis units) to Israel in February 1960. Oddly, in Israel, the model received the title Atlantean, presumably because that bus, a Leyland double-decker, had a similar rear-mounted engine. The two Lions for Israel were ready in January 1961. In May, Leyland announced that it had secured an order for twenty-five Lion buses for Dan, but the number was later reduced to twenty units, and came down to nothing when Dan chose to leave the Lions out of the deal and instead take delivery of ordinary Tigers. It was not a good sign and much to Leyland's disappointment, no Lions were sold at all in America, and as few as eighty-eight units – thirty in Australia, two in New Zealand, one in Spain and another one in Turkey, fifty-two in Iran and Israel's pair – were ordered, all told. The two Israeli Lions were taken out of service after ten years and sent to the scrapyard.

Leyland's presence in Israel had reached such a high level that a new Leyland assembly line was inaugurated in the port city of Ashdod, south of Tel Aviv, and the company achieved the status of a government-approved monopoly for the next several years, building trucks for the local market as well as buses that at one time were even exported to Romania. 'Leyland Ashdod' (52 per cent Leyland ownership, with the remaining 48 per cent held by an Israeli investor) was expected to have an annual output of 500 vehicles, but in 1963 it had already exceeded that number by turning out 515 vehicles, 250 of which were buses and the rest trucks. The factory was sold off in 1973 and, having been renamed as 'Ashdod Vehicle Works' (AVW), started building Mack trucks, of which 457 were manufactured in 1974, in addition to 238 Leyland trucks. AVW was closed down in 1984, under pressure from Mack and seven years following Leyland's departure from Israel.

The tense political situation in the Middle East, and especially Egypt's openly hostile policy towards Israel, led to the outbreak of the Six Day War, which took place in June 1967 and ended in Israel's sweeping territorial victory. Jordan, Syria and Egypt had all lost vast areas during the war, including east Jerusalem, the Samaria and Judea regions, the Golan Heights and all of Sinai. The combined effect of securing a new territory of such a large scale was a need for hundreds of new buses for public and private use. The unprecedented demand was partly met with new Leyland buses that were shipped, as chassis units, to Holland and Greece, where they were assembled and put back on a boat to Israel. However, by then the need for a new and better bus model for the Israeli market was becoming obvious, leading to the import of German-made MAN and Mercedes-Benz buses, and the difficulties encountered in getting spare parts from Leyland, due to the Arab Boycott on Israel (despite Leyland's strenuous denial), as well as Leyland's own production problems, only served to speed up the process of turning the final page on forty years of Leyland buses in Israel.

Preservation and Restoration

A few miles to the south of Tel Aviv, in the suburb of Holon and close to the Mediterranean Sea, is the Egged Heritage Center, whose collection of vintage trucks and buses is one of Israel's finest attractions. Kept in mint condition, and capable of pulling out of the center's main gate unassisted, the buses in the Leyland section have to be seen to be believed. With dozens of models representing Leyland's partnership with Israel, visitors young and old are invited to board the beautifully restored buses for a nostalgic ride into the past, and get a genuine hands-on experience of a fully functioning Royal Tiger bus. The center is also home to other Egged bus models, such as Mercedes-Benz city and long-haul buses from the 1970s and 1980s, the French Chausson, a Neoplan double-decker, and a jaw-dropping range of converted American trucks from the 1940s, all of them lovingly cared for in Egged's own bus garage.

Several Leyland buses have found their way to private hands in Israel, and a few surviving examples are proudly driven up and down the countryside to attend fan meetings and classic car shows and on special occasions, such as Israel's Independence Day celebrations in Jerusalem and Tel Aviv. Always the highlight of the show, they are a part of Israel's 'Leyland culture' and an automatic draw for countless Israelis whose childhood memories are firmly associated with the unmistakable sight and sound of the Leyland bus.

Unless otherwise stated, all photos are courtesy of the Egged Bus Archive, Jerusalem.

One of the highlights of the 1936 Levant Fair was a Leyland double-decker bus, which entered regular service with Hamaavir Bus Company in Tel Aviv. It was damaged during an Egyptian air raid on Tel Aviv on 17 May 1948, but was repaired and put back in service until finally retired in the early 1960s. (Library of Congress (Matson Collection), photo No. 18132)

Early examples of Leyland buses in Israel. Starting in 1949, a batch of Tiger model buses was ordered from Britain (as chassis units) using American foreign aid funds. With locally built bodies, these new Egged buses proved reliable and efficient to such a degree that additional orders were placed with Leyland in the coming years. Tiberias-bound bus No. 88-640 was photographed in a bus terminal in the 1950s, with its driver proudly posing for the camera.

Opposite page bottom, above, next page top, next page middle, next page bottom: A handful of Leyland buses existed in British Palestine prior to the establishment of the State of Israel. The change in Leyland's favour occurred after 1948, with the introduction of various truck models in Israel, including the Leyland Tiger. Forty-three Leyland chassis units were imported from Britain and, having been converted to buses, delivered to the main five Israeli public transport companies, to be used on their local and long-haul routes. These Leyland buses proved to be a success. Even better, Leyland parts were found to be compatible with other American and European bus models then present in Israel, meaning higher efficiency and reduced maintenance costs. However, a better model was needed, and accordingly, an Israeli delegation was dispatched to Britain to meet with the bus manufacturers there. Leyland's proposal, which was ultimately accepted, consisted of a mid-body engine bus (instead of the front-mounted version) holding fifty-one seats. Trial runs were held in Israel, with Leyland gaining the upper hand. Thus began the Leyland era in Israel, opening up the way for the purchase of thousands of Leyland Mark 1 and 2 buses and the creation of a Leyland bus and truck assembly line in Ashdod. It is a credit to Leyland that the last of the company's front-mounted engine buses were only retired by 1966, following a long and demanding career in Israel.

The reader's attention is drawn to Leyland bus No. M1187 (facing the right), which belonged to Derom Yehuda, a bus company that was created in 1931 and merged into Egged in 1951, at around the same time as the photo was taken. Originally linking the Jewish communities to the south of Tel Aviv, in the Second World War the company's services were retained to carry Polish servicemen between Iran, Syria and Egypt, and under vastly different circumstances, Jewish refugees coming from war-devastated Europe. In 1947, upon the end of the British Mandate in Palestine, the company's fleet consisted of Ford, Mack and White buses serving some 15,000 passengers daily. Leyland bus No. M1187 is seen here on a local journey to Givat Brenner, an agricultural community outside the city of Rehovot.

Despite its considerable success in Israel, Leyland was at first faced with strong competition from other British bus manufacturers who were eager to gain a steady foothold in a rapidly growing overseas market. One such competitor was the Associated Equipment Company, or AEC, who delivered several experimental chassis units with locally built bodies. Seen here in 1952 on an official rollout photo, a new AEC bus is ready to undergo a series of tests in Israel. The tests concluded, it was finally decided to place the order with Leyland, whose buses were found to be superior to AEC's. Ironically, AEC itself was taken over by Leyland in 1962 and vanished along with the parent company in 1979.

A new Leyland Mark 1 bus for Egged, freshly off the assembly line in Israel in 1955. Sporting the new 'rising wave' color scheme, these buses were certainly an elegant and eye-pleasing spectacle on the streets of Tel Aviv.

Old meets new in this photo of a Leyland Mark 1 bus on a local service in Tel Aviv, with an antiquated Mack bus to the left and a Leyland-DAB tourist class bus (painted in white) to the right.

Under construction in Israel, new Leyland Mark 1 buses are taking form in 1955. A simple and Spartan body design was chosen for that type, but this was gradually improved with later models.

Leyland Mark 1 No. M479 was one of two buses that were assembled in Israel in 1952 by Hamekasher, a Jerusalem-based bus company that was merged into Egged in 1967. Note the curiously placed side indicators, which were located under the windshield and consisted of two arrows, with each arrow pointing in a different direction.

A rather dramatic view of Leyland Mark 1 bus No. 38-725, showing two mechanics examining the underbody section in Egged's Azor garage, near Tel Aviv, which was recently closed down in favor of a new depot near Lydda.

A Haifa-bound Egged bus is packed – literally so – and set to depart from Tel Aviv Central station in 1961. Visible right below the Leyland emblem, between the headlights, is that of Haargaz (in Hebrew 'The Box'), one of two Israeli bus body manufacturers that were contracted to turn the Leyland chassis units into complete buses.

Rollout photo of Egged bus No. T2356. When introduced in Israel in the 1950s, these buses established a new service standard with their modern design and attractive look. Automatic doors were certainly a novelty, hence the warning (in Hebrew) near the front door 'Caution! Automatic door!'

The clean and eye-pleasing lines of Egged's Ness Ziona station are easy to see in this exciting lot of three colour photos from the early 1960s. Inaugurated in 1958, Ness Ziona (literally 'Carry the flag to Zion') station is located on the main road between Tel Aviv and Rehovot, with long-haul connections to Beersheba and Ashkelon. With the exception of the southbound, elderly-looking GMC bus, the rest are Leyland Mark 2 buses operating on various local routes, all wearing the Egged colors of the period.

The changing times in Israel in this 1950s view of an Egged garage in Haifa. Occupying the spacious shed is a French Chausson, with its sun visor, and over the adjacent pit, a freshly painted Leyland Royal Tiger Mark 2. The Chaussons did not last long in Israel and whereas Egged's affair with Chausson was short-lived, excellent business ties were maintained with the British bus manufacturer.

Still carrying the old four-digit registration plates, six Egged buses are seen on a Sukkot (the Feast of Tabernacles) Special day trip in 1958. Third in the line is an Egged Tours bus, easily recognised with its see-through roof windows and different colors and markings. Public events such as this were instrumental in the formation of a Leyland culture in Israel.

A bird's-eye view of the central bus station in downtown Tel Aviv in the early 1960s. A paradise for Leyland fans, Royal Tigers are clearly dominating the narrow platforms, with but a single nose-mounted veteran bus in the crowded, Leyland-only yard. The color variations between Egged, on the right, and Dan, in the middle, are obvious.

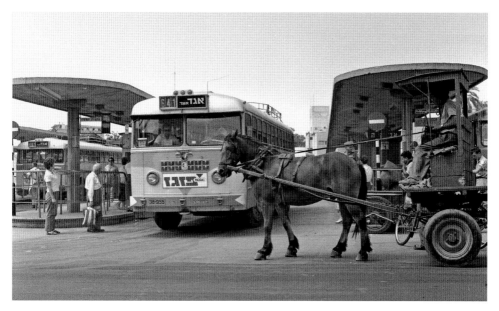

In 1961, when this photo was taken, horse-drawn carts were a common sight on the streets of Tel Aviv. Egged bus No. 38-955, a Leyland Mark 2, is scheduled to depart with the 641 suburban service to what back then used to be a few rural communities outside the city, and have since then fallen victim to the inevitable urban sprawl. Ironically, with the heavy traffic in metropolitan Tel Aviv, the average speed today is often as low as that attained by the same horse-drawn cart more than half a century ago!

The Judean hills provide a picturesque setting for this photo of an Egged bus struggling up the steep climb to Jerusalem in the 1950s. The location is Motza, only a few miles to the west of Jerusalem. The whole area is completely changed today and the single-lane road has long since been replaced with a wide new highway, including several bridges and tunnels.

A warm and sunny day, a holiday at the beach and a Leyland bus all make this photo a sweet childhood memory for a good many Israelis who were fortunate enough to grow up in the 1960s. Egged bus No. 38-808 has brought a group of summer camp holidaymakers for a swim in the sea, near Tel Aviv, and is apparently about to dip its own feet in the water!

Tel Aviv Central station in 1961. A 1956-built Dan Leyland Mark 2, on a local service, is passing in front of another Dan bus, in this case a Dodge. Both buses are now a distant memory at best, having long since been replaced with German-made MAN buses. Eco-friendly electric buses are gradually entering service with Dan at this time.

Somewhere in the desolate Negev Desert in 1959, Egged bus No. 2765 makes its way to Israel's southern tip on the Red Sea, on the occasion of the port city of Eilat's tenth anniversary. A remote settlement in those days, Eilat has since then grown into the holiday capital of Israel and the gateway to Sinai and Egypt, with an international airport and regular bus connections to all parts of the country.

Official portrait of the Leyland Royal Tiger Mark 2 bus chassis, prior to delivery to Israel and with the engine and mechanical parts already assembled.

General Photos of Leyland Buses at Work in Israel

Egged bus No. 2588 was a Leyland Mark 2 built in 1956. The large sign 'Tel Aviv Direct' might explain the amusing drawing of a small plane near the right-side headlight!

Egged bus No. 917 was a 1955 Leyland Mark 1. The exact location of this photo is unknown, but could be somewhere in the north of Israel.

The Italian-made Ceccato automatic bus wash was a major improvement in the regular daily care and overall cleanliness of all public buses. Egged bus No. 2777 is taking a shower in a photo dated to 1959, in Tel Aviv, after completing the long journey from Beersheba.

Another Leyland Mark 2 captured on film was bus No. 2840, which was delivered to Egged in 1958. With a partial view of a GMC bus to the left and a Chausson bus to the right, this photo seems to encapsulate the shape of things to come over the next several decades, with Leyland's successful takeover of the Israeli bus market.

A few miles to the east of Tel Aviv is Petah Tikva, a Jewish agricultural colony established in 1878 and today a bustling suburb in metropolitan Tel Aviv. In a photo believed to have been taken in 1958, Leyland-built Egged bus No. 2882 is carrying a large banner announcing the inauguration of the new Petah Tikva bus station, as is the next bus to the right. As of 2020, the new Tel Aviv Metro is expected to reach Petah Tikva soon, considerably reducing the total travel time when compared with the road traffic along the same route.

The sunlight is brightly reflected on the front of Egged bus No. 3027, in a photo dated 1 October 1958 and possibly taken during the same Sukkot Special day trip depicted in photo No. 18. Parked in the background are two other buses – a Leyland and a British Daimler.

Egged bus No. 3097 was a Leyland Mark 2 built in 1958, here seen at the company's Rosh Pinna garage in downtown Tel Aviv in the 1960s. Both bus and garage have long since vanished into history; a modern glass-plated office building now stands on the same site of the old garage. The purpose of the digit '3' on the bus is unclear, although one is amusingly tempted to think of it as denoting the level of comfort – that is, third class.

Official Egged publicity photo of a 1958-built Leyland bus in Tel Aviv, ready to depart the station on a clear and sunny day. Ventilation, always in demand in the merciless tropical Israeli summer, was still a rare luxury in those days, and was only made possible thanks to drop-down side windows along the bus.

Keeping things in order was once the travelling controller's duty. In this color photo from the 1960s, Egged bus No. 38-701 is having its wheels checked during a springtime day trip into the countryside. Radio communication was the standard method of keeping in touch with the depot, long before the invention of the mobile phone and the Internet.

The idea of spending anything up to four to five hours aboard an old bus is hard to imagine when compared with any of the modern, air-conditioned models of today. Yet, fifty years ago, this Leyland bus was standard equipment on route No. 841, running routinely on the long journey from Tel Aviv to Kiryat Shmona (Israel's northernmost city). Leyland bus No. 37-752, called 'Lark' in Egged, is taking a wash after the challenging uphill climb to the Upper Galilee.

In a scene requiring little explanation, Egged's 1,000th Leyland Mark 2 bus is officially presented in public and, ready to receive its first ever passengers, inaugurated into regular public service in Jerusalem Central on 9 August 1965.

A team of Egged mechanics is carefully inspecting the diesel motor of a Leyland bus in the company's spacious Haifa garage. Massive hydraulic jacks have replaced the old pits, permitting easy access to all parts of any bus in the company's fleet.

Compare the view of the modern Haifa garage in the previous photo with this one, showing the old bus depot in Tel Aviv. Two Leylands, a Mark 1 and a Mark 2, are standing next to a GMC bus, and are waiting for what appears to be an oil inspection.

תור
טייל
בארץ

"אגד" (א.ש.ה.)

באוטובוסים מיוחדים

An Egged Tours Leyland Mark 1 bus is at the center of this vintage 'explore Israel' postcard celebrating the new and comfortable way to discover the wonders of the Holy Land. As will be noted in the following photos, the new Leyland buses were central to Israel's growing tourism industry, setting a higher service standard immediately upon their arrival.

Previous page bottom, above, below & opposite page: These rare color photos are exceptionally helpful in appreciating the difference between Egged's tourist class Leyland and Daimler buses. Both types were imported from Britain as chassis units and assembled in Israel, however according to different specifications and dimensions. They are here seen 'on the job' during visits to romantic destinations in Israel, such as Caesarea and the Negev Desert.

Official portrait of a British Daimler Freeline bus, as delivered to Egged in 1958. Ironically, despite their overall high quality, the Daimlers had their original diesel motors replaced with Leyland ones. They did not last long in service and sadly none of the Daimlers were preserved.

Egged bus No. 39-557 was another tourist class Leyland assembled in Israel, according to a design issued by the Merkavim Metal Works. Black basalt bricks, seen in the background, are common to the Sea of Galilee area. The location of this photo is Capernaum in the 1960s.

The blue water of the Sea of Galilee provides the background for this 1970s view of an Egged bus travelling through a quiet street in Tiberias. Palm trees are a common sight throughout the entire Jordan Valley, whose hot climate is ideal for the growth of the finest dates. (Author's collection)

The colorful market in Beersheba is popular with visitors from near and afar. In a romantic scene, two camels – one real, the other built by Leyland and operated by Egged – are eyeing each other outside a typical Bedouin tent. (Author's collection)

The desert city of Arad is conveniently located near the UNESCO World Heritage Site of Masada, which is an ancient fortress located on a breathtaking plateau high above the Dead Sea. A Dan Tours Leyland bus, in red, white and blue, is the focal point of this view of the still empty city center. (Author's collection)

Neatly parked along the side of a cruise liner, four Egged Tours buses – three Leylands and a single Daimler – are ready to head out of the Port of Haifa on an organized tour of Israel. A similar 'sail and rail' service was provided within the same years for visitors wishing to make the journey from Haifa to Jerusalem by a self-propelled diesel train.

The Old City of Jerusalem is a labyrinth of tiny alleys and narrow roads, and hardly a place for a bus. Despite that, Egged bus No. 66-329 makes it safely through the extremely limited space with the Wailing Wall local service in a photo from the 1970s. A second bus is trailing right behind, down the same road, presumably with fingers crossed against any sudden mechanical problems and no way to overtake the leading bus!

In a scene that was once standard all over Israel, a Leyland 'Lark' is seen at a bus stop on a scheduled local service in Haifa in the 1960s.

Above, below & next page above below: Four official Leyland-DAB photos showing the Danish manufacturer's buses in Frederikshavns Omnibiler and other color schemes. Essentially a Leyland bus chassis supporting a Danish-built body, a few were exported to Israel in the early 1960s. With their beautiful colors, the illustrated models will certainly appeal to any Leyland fan.

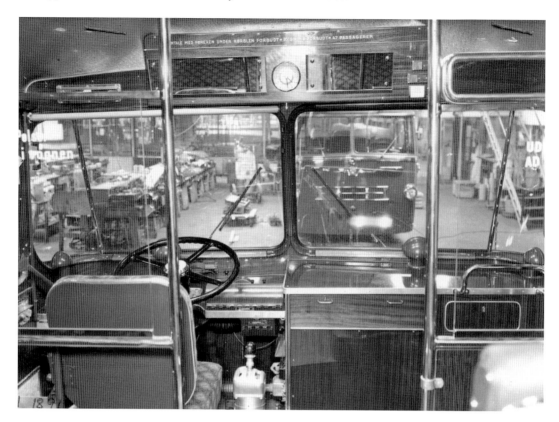

Up to seven Leyland-DAB buses were sold to Hamekasher Bus Company, including this one for the Jerusalem local service. The company was merged with Egged in 1967, only a few years later. This bus is believed to have been retired in 1976.

The large inscription in Hebrew 'Jet Queens – Guests of Egged Tours' stands out in this 1964 photo of Leyland-DAB bus No. 39-261 on a flight attendants' trip to Jerusalem. Mounted on the roof is another inscription greeting bus and air passengers. In the distance, to the right, are the Mount of Olives and the Russian Church and Tower of the Ascension in east Jerusalem.

A busy street scene in the 1960s, with Dan buses running up and down Allenby Street near the central bus station in downtown Tel Aviv. A tiny BMW Isetta seems to look on with interest! (Author's collection)

A batch of Leyland tourist class buses was ordered in 1963 from the Greek coachbuilder Biamax (BIAMAΞ, pronounced 'Viamax') due to a sharp rise in the general demand for more buses in Israel and the production limits of the local suppliers. As an added bonus, it was discovered that the Greek Leylands were considerably cheaper and far more luxurious than the ones previously assembled in Israel. They were equipped with a double floor for engine noise reduction, a protective double roof against the heat outside the bus, ventilation holes and comfortable seats. These buses were retired after a decade in service.

Right & Below: With their gentle curves and elegant design, the Biamax Leylands were easily some of the prettiest buses in Egged's fleet. The round windshield and double headlights over a shining front bumper only added to their stately look. The presence of an air conditioner must have been a huge relief for both passengers and driver alike in the blistering summer heat.

For the 36th International Public Transportation Congress, which was held in Israel in 1965, a single Leyland Viberty demonstrator bus was temporarily delivered to Egged for a series of tests. At 17 metres, this articulated bus had seventy-six seats and originally a right-hand steering wheel, which was moved to the left side in Leyland's own Ashdod works. It was used briefly in the Tel Aviv area and, having been returned to Leyland's agent in Israel, is said to have been scrapped after several years in storage.

Officine Viberti of Turin was an Italian manufacturer of trailers and buses, as well as mopeds and military vehicles. Between 1955 and 1957, it cooperated with the German motorcycle manufacturer Victoria. It now belongs to a Polish business consortium.

A look inside the Egged garage near Tel Aviv in the 1960s, with three Leyland Mark 2 buses occupying the maintenance stations inside the main hall.

A 1980s view of Egged bus No. 37-655 on a scheduled local service somewhere along Jaffa Road in central Jerusalem. Fit as ever despite their age, these elderly Leylands were replaced by newer Mercedes-Benz buses. Electric streetcars now run along Jaffa Road, and no buses are allowed there anymore.

Inauguration of the new Tel Aviv–Eilat route on 30 August 1964. Egged bus No. 39-512 is seen on the first day of service.

The elegant colors of this Dan bus are hard to miss in this photo of Tel Aviv in the 1960s. At one time a major Leyland customer in Israel, the Dan Leylands enjoyed a stylish color design for the first several years of their regular service.

This page & next page: In the Six Day War of June 1967, the Kingdom of Jordan had lost all of its territories to the west of the Jordan River, including Jerusalem and the Samaria and Judea regions. A political turning point in the history of the Middle East, Israel's triumph over her Arab neighbors led to a massive rise in the tourism traffic to the newly acquired lands. The beautiful biblical hills outside Jerusalem soon became a huge draw for visitors, with a good choice of historical and archaeological sites dating back to the days of the Roman and Ottoman empires. On a clear summer's day, two Egged buses are travelling on the Jerusalem–Samaria main road on a sightseeing trip of the Holy Land.

The term 'all-terrain vehicle' comes to mind upon the first look at this early 1970s photo of Egged bus No. 89-769 struggling up the muddy dirt road to the ancient fortress of Sartaba, in the eastern Samaria and overlooking the Jordan Valley.

Opposite page above below, this page above below & next page above below: Another outcome of Israel's sweeping victory in the Six Day War of June 1967 was the complete takeover of the Sinai Peninsula from Egypt and the creation of new long-haul bus routes to civilian and military destinations in the deep desert. Getting around Sinai, despite the availability of properly paved roads, sometimes required a journey off the main road, and through some of the most spectacular landscape imaginable. It was in this rough and rugged wasteland that the Leylands were able to fully demonstrate their strength, negotiating extremely tight turns and travelling over difficult dirt roads to such remote places as Mount Sinai and Saint Catherine's Monastery. It is a credit to Leyland that their buses performed faultlessly even under such challenging conditions, and with complete satisfaction. Egged buses Nos 39-288 and 38-571 are seen on a tour of Sinai in the 1970s. Israel has since then returned the peninsula to Egypt, in the 1979 peace agreement, turning the final page on a decade of regular bus tours of Sinai.

Looking resplendent in this official photo is an Egged Tours Leyland bus standing next to a pair of DC-3 Dakota planes belonging to the Israeli airline Arkia. A time-saving, combined air and road service was established in the 1960s to carry passengers to Masada. The same arrangement appears to have been maintained also in the north of Israel for a few years.

Previous page below, this page abve & below: 225 Van Hool/Leyland buses were delivered complete to Israel in the early 1970s for Egged's local and long-haul routes. These photos show the new buses immediately upon arrival in Israel, with the distinctive 'lantern screen' windshield. In Israel, they lasted for some twenty years in regular service and two buses are preserved.

On a busy morning outside the Egged and Dan Tours travel office on No. 8 Mendeli Street in western Tel Aviv, eight beautifully painted Dan and Egged Tours Leyland buses are all set to pull out of the city to destinations across Israel. Today this address is a short walk from the British Embassy in Israel.

In 1973, Egged decided to paint its long-haul and tourist class buses in bright red, with the rest of the fleet, that is buses for local services, in blue. This photo demonstrates the two color options, while also showing the clever use of white stripes along the entire length of the body.

Many of the Leyland buses in Israel were routinely taken over by the army in times of war, and sent out to the front lines in the far north and south of the country. A Leyland bus belonging to Egged Tours seems relaxed in the company of two Centurion tanks, somewhere in the Golan Heights in 1973.

With its headlights blacked out, Egged bus No. 39-315 is passing through a military checkpoint close to the Israeli-Syrian border in June 1967. This photo was taken near the Syrian town of Quneitra, which was situated on the main road to Damascus and was under Israeli military control until 1974.

The Israeli crossing of the Suez Canal during the Yom Kippur War of October 1973 was made possible using a barge bridge, opening the way into Egypt. Hundreds of buses were hastily sent down to Sinai, where they remained in military service for several months and right up to the cessation of all hostilities. This photo shows an Egged Tours Leyland bus advancing carefully over the water during the war.

The blue sky is reflected in the Suez Canal in this late summer photo of two Egged buses in Sinai during the 1973 war. Military traffic on the bridge was intense, and no fewer than 2,600 Leyland buses were needed to meet the total military demand in Israel's difficult and ultimately successful fight against her invading Arab neighbours.

Egged bus No. 89-693 was sent to the white sands of Sinai in 1973. A Centurion tank is about to be deployed off a trailer to the left. Both tank and bus are of British origin. The bus is a Royal Tiger Mark 2 built by Leyland, as were some of the first Centurions. (Photo: Chaim Avni)

'Goodbye, Africa!' An Egged Tours bus on the way out of Sinai in 1974 with a homebound military convoy after a long and hard campaign in the dusty desert along the Suez Canal. Only a few years later, in March 1979, Israel and Egypt signed a peace agreement, and a direct Tel Aviv–Cairo bus line was established using four new Mercedes-Benz O303 buses that were delivered to Egged in 1982.

Previous page below, this page above below & opposite page above below: In the early 1980s, in response to Palestinian terror attacks on civilian targets in northern Israel, a large-scale military campaign was launched in an attempt to drive the PLO out of Beirut and all of Lebanon. Egged and Dan buses were once more called in to assist with the war effort and, as illustrated in these photos from 1982, were dispatched all the way to the front line, often in military convoys.

Official photo of the Leyland Lion bus chassis, two examples of which were delivered to Israel in the early 1960s. Partly seen behind the large plate is the rear-mounted diesel engine, which was peculiarly housed in a fibreglass compartment, well outside the back of the bus. The Lion was unpopular with the Israeli bus companies and no orders were placed with Leyland for that model.

Above & below: Several Leyland buses ended up with private Israeli operators. The Nazareth-based Hagalil Bus Company owned a few Royal Tigers and ran them regularly in public service to Haifa.

No. 38-488 may seem to be an ordinary Egged bus. It was in fact anything but that. Originally a Leyland Mark 2 assembled in Greece and delivered complete to Israel in 1971, in 1979 it was rebuilt and returned to regular service with a new Israeli-made body. This bus was withdrawn in the 1980s but a similar model, No. 39-486, is on display at Egged's Heritage Center.

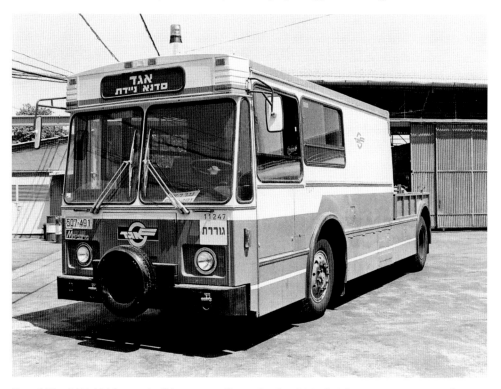

Egged No. 507-491 began its life as an ordinary Leyland Mark 2 bus. It was converted into a tow truck in the early 1980s, in keeping with the company's cost-cutting policy of using its own buses for such non-standard purposes as parts carriers and mobile workshops.

Phasing out of the Leyland buses in Egged took place in the 1980s, simultaneously with the introduction of new Mercedes-Benz O303s. Egged bus No. 88-022 is parked next to a recent arrival from Germany.

Egged Visitor's Center – Preserved Leyland Buses

Above & below: Israel's oldest surviving Leyland bus was delivered new in 1949, as part of a batch of thirty units ordered on short notice from the British manufacturer. With only thirty-seven seats and a nose-mounted 150 hp engine, it was technically a short-term solution until the arrival of a better Leyland model. However, these buses lasted into the 1960s and were retired after many years in service. Bus No. T1254 was used mostly in the Haifa Bay area and, upon retirement in November 1967, was stationed afoot the snow-capped Mount Hermon, overlooking the Golan Heights.

Above, next page above & below: 'Leyland Row' is a fitting name for these retired Egged buses, which are parked within the Visitor's Center's grounds. Once the backbone of Israel's public transport system, these last few survivors are living remnants of what may rightfully, and certainly sentimentally, be called the Leyland era in Israel.

Originally a 1958 Leyland bus, this 'homemade' Egged mobile workshop is powered by a six-cylinder, 168 hp engine. No. 507-471 was assigned to the company's Ashkelon depot, to the south of Tel Aviv. It has since then been replaced with converted Mercedes-Benz and MAN buses that were similarly removed from active service and given garage duties.

Royal Tiger Mark 2 bus No. 37-918 was built in 1968, at the height of Israel's affair with Leyland. Hundreds of these buses were sold to Egged over the years, and they were among the last to have remained in regular use until the arrival of new German-made buses.

This page & opposite page: Egged bus No. 88-894 is one of one of 300 Mark 2 units built for service in Israel in the 1950s.

Egged bus No. T2435 is a Leyland bus whose body had been assembled at Haargaz Works in Israel. On entering service in 1956, it was allocated to the Tiberias area, near the Sea of Galilee. Post-1967, it served as a driving school bus in Jerusalem and has since then been handed over to the company's Visitor's Center for preservation.

Proudly displayed in Egged's Visitor's Center near Tel Aviv, these lovingly restored Leyland veterans are kept in mint condition and in full running order.

Standing shoulder to shoulder, these two locally assembled Leyland Mark 2 buses were delivered to Egged in the 1960s. With their impressive double headlights and well-proportioned design, they represent the golden age of Leyland in Israel. Of special interest is bus No. 38-153 (nicknamed 'Safari') whose upper body had been professionally removed for the annual Purim carnival. As its name suggests, it was meant to carry visitors inside the Safari Zoo, near Tel Aviv; however, it was never used there at all.

Other than buses, the collection also includes a Leyland Beaver truck, painted in bright blue. In service from 1962 to the late 1980s, truck No. 103-581 was assembled in Leyland's Ashdod Works, in Israel, and was used exclusively to haul diesel fuel to Egged's own depots. It was powered by a six-cylinder Leyland engine delivering a modest 168 hp.

The bare chassis of Egged bus No. 89-773, a Royal Tiger Mark 2, showing Leyland's ingeniously simple and solid design, which, in Israel's case, was replicated in the hundreds. The location of the diesel engine was right at the center, between the front and rear wheels.

Egged bus No. 337-722 was originally designed for local and suburban services, with its wide back doors. However, in the October 1973 war (also known as the Yom Kippur War) it was recruited by the army and in its new role in military service, was converted to a large ambulance – one of several such buses that ended up near the front line in the Sinai Desert and the Golan Heights.

Bus No. 38-023 was a relatively late Royal Tiger Mark 2 model. Commonly called 'Lark' in Egged, it was one of only thirty units assembled in Israel in 1969, with forty-seven seats and the usual 168 hp engine. It was similarly among the last Leyland buses to be retired in the late 1980s.

One of twenty units of this type that were assembled in Israel in 1957, tourist class bus No. 66-064 had thirty-nine seats and originally belonged to the Jerusalem-based Hamekasher Bus Company. Merged with Egged in 1967, Hamekasher ceased to exist and this bus, which was ordered specifically for Israel's tenth Independence Day, ended up with Egged's driving school. It was retired in the 1980s.

With its classic Van Hool front and windshield design, Egged bus No. 38-327 was imported to Israel complete in 1970 as part of an order for 225 Leyland buses (seventy-five units for short and another 150 for long-haul routes).

Above & opposite page: Introduced in 1968, Egged Tours bus No. 89-299 could not have arrived at a more appropriate time than Israel's military victory over her Arab neighbors in the Six Day War of June 1967. With Sinai, the Golan Heights and the entire land to the west of the Jordan River in Israeli hands, this upgraded Leyland bus was the right answer for the rapid growth both in the number of tourists travelling in Israel, as well as the total traffic volume in the new territories. The first air-conditioned bus with an independent climate control unit, this bus also had forty-three seats and a fibreglass front.

As many as 700 units of this Leyland Royal Tiger Mark 2 model were supplied to Egged through the years for local services. Bus No. 37-659 was built in 1970 and remained in regular use for twenty years. A simple design, the type rightfully deserves the title of one of Egged's most popular Leyland buses.

Twenty Leyland buses were ordered in 1971 from Saracakis of Greece. They were mechanically identical to any other Royal Tiger Mark 2 already present in Israel, with the usual 168 hp, six-cylinder engine, and had a relatively short career in Israel of only thirteen years.

On first view, Egged bus No. 39-486 is a standard Leyland Royal Tiger Mark 2 built in 1970. However, along with fourteen other Egged buses, the original bodies were removed and replaced with new coach class bodies, using the same original chassis.

The amusing name 'Aquarium Class' becomes clear upon the first look at the peculiar windshield shape of Egged bus No. 66-348 (Leyland 1962). With its bulging windows, presumably so built for better visibility, it was one of forty-five buses operated by Hamekasher in Jerusalem. The class remained there post-merger with Egged, and was retired after twenty-one years in service.

Above & below: Of all the many Leyland buses in the collection, the prettiest of them all in the author's opinion is No. 39-430, which was built in 1963. Bringing together form and functionality, and with its beautiful double headlights and charming livery, hundreds of this type were delivered to Egged and, for the next twenty-three years, were present in all parts of Israel.

Ten experimental Leyland buses were delivered to Egged in 1967, where they were called Panthers. Equipped with air cushions and an upright, rear-mounted Leyland engine, they lasted for fifteen years with the company. Interestingly, post-Leyland era orders resulted in the arrival of Daimler Benz buses that had air suspension and an upright diesel engine that was placed at the back of the bus.

Despite its boxy and modern look, Egged bus No. 89-785 is actually a 1969 Leyland Mark 2 chassis supporting a locally built 1981 body. Named 'Moledet' ('Homeland'), this class consisted of forty buses that were specifically reserved for school trips. In reality, they proved too heavy for such use and were little used.

Above & below: Awaiting the cutter's torch in this late 1980s view of the so-called 'Leyland cemetery' near Erez are retired Egged buses. The sand dunes outside Gaza were the final resting place for countless Leyland buses, and a Palestinian workforce was recruited to dismantle each and every single one of them. Spare parts for Egged's Heritage Center near Tel Aviv were also sourced from the scrapped buses.

Up in the air goes an Egged Leyland bus, as it is being carefully loaded onto a ship on the long voyage from Israel to its new home in distant Myanmar. The front of another Burma-bound Leyland bus is partly visible to the right.

Above & below: A relatively large order for retired Egged buses arrived from Sierra Leone's Bus Transportation Company, who received the Leyland buses here seen in Erez, just outside the Gaza Strip, in 1989. Curiously, the new color scheme of green, white and blue resembled that once used by El Al, the Israeli airline, who also operated a few Leyland buses mostly in the Tel Aviv metropolitan area.

Once an Egged bus, this Royal Tiger was sold to a Nigerian operator and is here seen repainted in white and blue, prior to shipment from Israel to its new home in the former British colony in Africa. The company's name 'Ekene Dili Chukwu' is translated into 'Thanks to God' and differs slightly from that applied to the bus.

The iconic 'Charging Tiger' emblem. Proudly carried on Israel's countless Royal Tiger buses, it is today little more than a nostalgic reminder from bygone times in Leyland's own history, as well as a sentimental childhood memory for those among us who were young enough to recall the immense joy of discovering the world outside the window of a travelling Tiger bus.

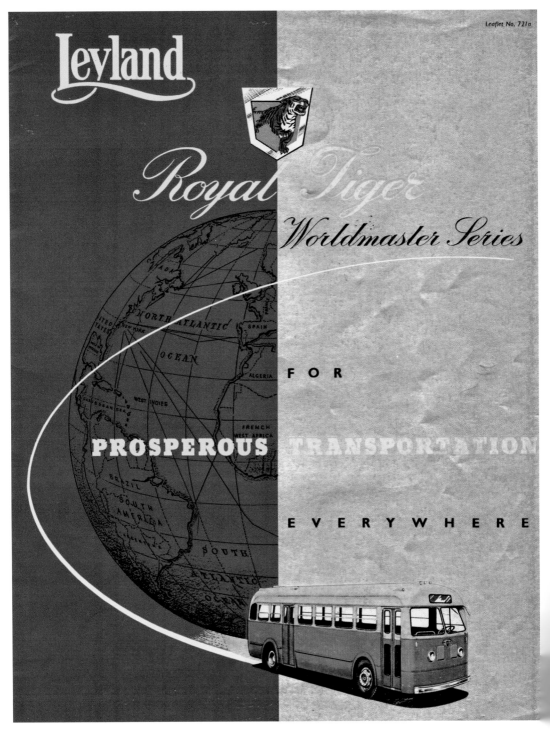

'For prosperous transportation everywhere!' This is the front page of the Leyland Royal Tiger Worldmaster Series sales brochure from 1954, describing the model's many technical advantages and overall superiority over other bus manufacturers.

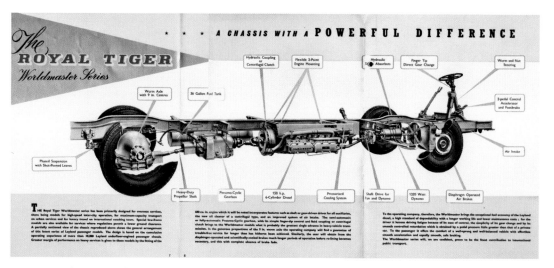

From the same sales brochure, a detailed color illustration showing the Leyland Royal Tiger bus chassis and various components.

Built in Greece, bus No. 38-537 was one of thirty-five deluxe class Leylands that were delivered new to Egged Tours. On a clear summer day, this bus is about to collect its passengers from one of the large hotels in Tel Aviv. Partly visible in the background, over the blue Mediterranean Sea, is western Jaffa.

In 1942, the British-built Cairo–Haifa railway line was extended northwards along the coastline into western Lebanon. LMS Class 8F and other British-built steam locomotives were routinely assigned to haul supply trains from Lebanon to Egypt during the Second World War. Essentially a military railway, the new Haifa–Beirut–Tripoli line survived the war and inspiring post-war plans were made to run passenger trains between Egypt and Turkey along the same route. Sadly, politics got in the way and by 1948 the service between Israel and Lebanon came to a complete and final stop. In a photo from the 1970s, Egged bus No. 38-561 stands right on the abandoned track leading into one of the railway tunnels at Rosh Hanikra (in Hebrew 'Head of the Grotto'), on the Israeli side of the border with Lebanon. A cable car is used to carry visitors to the base of the imposing Rosh Hanikra limestone cliff.